LEE EVANS
TOPICS
in
JAZZ and MUSICAL CREATIVITY

for the
Classical Pianist

MW00669008

CONTENTS

Piano Plus, inc.

EXCLUSIVELY DISTRIBUTED BY

HAL•LEONARD®
CORPORATION
7777 W. BLUEMOUND RD. P.O. BOX 13819 MILWAUKEE, WI 53213

Understanding Chord Symbols

BY LEE EVANS

Classical pianists are often intimidated by alphabetical chord symbols used in popular music and jazz. They may simply be unfamiliar with them, or may be bewildered by the confusing array of chord symbols in use and by common inconsistencies and errors in usage. They may also be uncomfortable with the improvisatory nature of playing from chord symbols.

A chord symbol never indicates voicing (the spacing of chord tones);

nor do chord symbols always indicate the use of inversions to create smoother voice leading. In playing from chord symbols, you must do more than merely play root position chords. Good voice leading mixes root positions and inversions to minimize leaps between corresponding voices of consecutive chords.

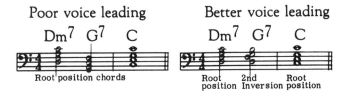

In interpreting chord symbols you should keep voice-leading considerations in mind at all times. Given sufficient practice and playing experience, using inversions becomes automatic.

No one system of chord symbol notation is universally accepted. Notational practice among composers, arrangers, and copyists continues to vary widely, and any attempt to define a standardized system is unlikely to gain universal acceptance. For example, all of the following chord symbols represent the same major seventh chord:

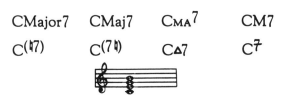

Lee Evans graduated from New York University and received his Master of Arts and Doctor of Education from Columbia University. Evans, who has taught music at the junior high, high school, and college levels, plays solo piano, performs with his orchestra, and acts as pianist and musical coordinator for such performers as Tom Jones, Carol Channing, and Emerson, Lake and Palmer. He is the author of a comprehensive series of books that teach jazz to classical pianists.

Because of the lack of uniformity in popular sheet music and fakebooks, it is important to be familiar with all of the most frequently used notational systems. The one basic principle is that the symbol for a given chord includes the letter name of the root of the chord.

Triads

Chord symbol notation for a major triad is a capital letter (the chord root). This also applies to a four-note major chord, with the root doubled at the octave.

A minor triad or four-note chord is represented by any of the following symbols:

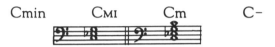

The three-note diminished triad occurs diatonically as the chord built on the seventh degree of the major scale. It is intervallically identical to a minor triad with flatted fifth.

The diminished chord occurs most frequently in jazz as a four-note chord, the seventh of the chord being a diminished seventh — often spelled as a major sixth — above the root. The symbols for a diminished seventh chord on C are:

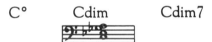

The normal resolution of the diminished seventh chord built on the seventh scale degree is to the tonic. In that respect it functions like a dominant seventh chord, whose normal resolution is also to the tonic. Because all adjacent tones of a diminished seventh chord are the same distance apart (a minor third), any one of its tones may be thought of as the root; thus in its root position and three inversions it can resolve to the tonic of four different major keys (or their parallel minor keys).

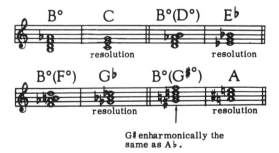

G♯ enharmonically the same as A♭.

An augmented triad is created by raising the fifth degree of a major triad by a half step; augmented triads thus contain all major thirds.

A plus sign, indicating a raised fifth, is generally used with the letter name of the root to represent augmented chords.

C+   Caug   C+5   C 5+

Seventh Chords

A dominant seventh chord is formed diatonically by adding a minor seventh above the root of the major triad built on the fifth degree of a major or minor scale. The term dominant seventh is generally used for any chord consisting of a major triad with a minor seventh, regardless of whether or not it is built on the fifth scale degree. The chord symbol is the letter name of the chord root and a 7:

G⁷   G7

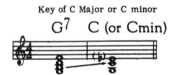

Note that the dominant seventh contains the interval of a diminished fifth (here, B to F), enharmonically the same as an augmented fourth or tritone (three whole steps). A dominant seventh chord, in traditional classical harmony and often in jazz, resolves to its respective tonic chord, with the leading tone moving up to the tonic.

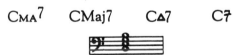

A major seventh chord consists of a major triad plus a major seventh above the chord root. Occasionally a major seventh is indicated by a 7 with a slash through it.

CMA⁷   CMaj7   CΔ7   C7̸

A minor seventh chord consists of a minor triad plus a minor seventh above the chord root.

CMI⁷   Cm7   Cmin7   C–7

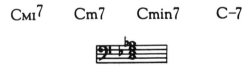

The symbol for a minor seventh chord with a major seventh above the root usually includes a natural or sharp sign to indicate the raised seventh.

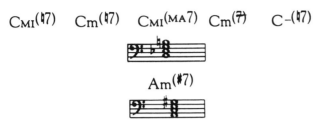

A half-diminished seventh chord consists of a diminished triad plus a minor seventh above the chord root.

This chord is equivalent to a minor seventh chord with lowered fifth, and is more frequently symbolized as such; this better reflects the chord's usual circle-of-fifths resolution expectation.

Other Chords

Sixth chords contain a triad plus a major sixth above the chord root. In a major sixth chord the triad is major; in a minor sixth chord the triad is minor, but the sixth is still major.

Note that in third inversion the major sixth chord is identical to the root position minor seventh chord.

Chord symbols can indicate the alteration of one or more tones of a chord; these alterations often appear in parentheses.

In chords with more than one altered tone the higher tone appears on top within the parentheses.

Omitted tones are usually written out.

The same is true of added tones. A major or minor triad with an added ninth – a major ninth, unless indicated otherwise – is symbolized as follows:

A sixth chord with added ninth, however, is represented by

A major, minor, or dominant ninth chord adds a ninth – major unless otherwise indicated – above the root of a major, minor, or dominant seventh chord.

Suspensions

A suspension is a non-harmonic tone – a tone not belonging to the chord – that usually resolves to a harmonic tone. In jazz harmony a suspension usually replaces the third of a triad with a major second or perfect fourth above the root. The normal resolution of the suspension is then to the third, either major or minor.

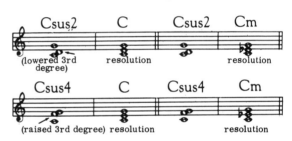

When the chord symbol for a suspension is not followed by a number (as in C sus), this generally indicates a sus 4. Occasionally a suspension will be notated as the chord name plus an Arabic numeral, omitting the sus abbreviation (C4 = Csus4).

Slash Marks

In recent years it has become common practice for arrangers and composers to indicate chord inversions, non-harmonic bass tones, and polychords through the use of horizontal or diagonal slash marks.

The character above or to the left of the slash represents the fundamental chord, and the character below or to the right of the slash represents the lowest tone of the chord or the bass note to be played by the left hand. This notational system is useful because, by indicating the inversion, the composer or arranger can suggest preferred voice leading.

A non-harmonic bass tone is similarly notated. If the following chord were symbolized as D♭maj7, a pianist would be unlikely to guess the composer's intentions.

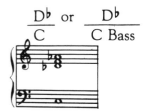

When a chord quality (major, minor, diminished, or augmented) and/or an Arabic numeral is indicated next to the character below or to the right of the slash, an entire chord rather than a single tone is to be played by the left hand while the right hand plays the chord indicated by the upper or left character.

This method of notating polychords is much clearer than indicating harmonic alterations.

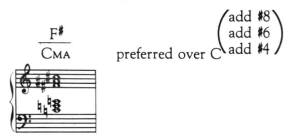

Eleventh and Thirteenth Chords

Eleventh chords are often symbolized by slash marks. This is particularly apt when, as is often the case in jazz, the third is omitted from the eleventh chord.

Similarly, slash mark notation is sometimes used in place of the sus abbreviation to indicate suspensions.

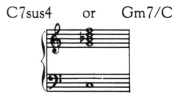

Thus in jazz usage eleventh chord notation (C11), slash mark notation (Gm7/C or B♭/C), and suspension notation (C7sus4) are used interchangeably; all three symbols represent the same chord.

A thirteenth chord theoretically indicates a seven-note chord. In jazz practice it is usually played as a four-note chord, omitting the fifth, ninth, and eleventh, or as a five-note chord, omitting the fifth and eleventh.

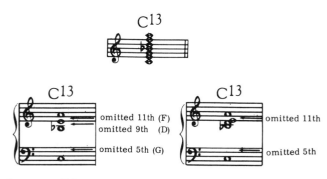

Incorrect Usage

Be alert to incorrect chord symbol usage in sheet music; often the symbol erroneously takes into account only what the right hand is playing.

Jazz musicians, who traditionally think of chords as being built upwards in thirds, regard altered notes as chromatic alterations of those thirds. Thus most jazz texts and jazz musicians refer to a dominant seventh with flatted tenth as a sharp ninth chord. Spelling the note as a lowered tenth is more accurate, even in jazz.

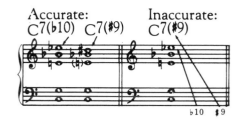

A chord symbol should account for the presence of every note in a chord. The best symbol to use in writing is the least complicated one — the one that is easiest to read and interpret at the keyboard. Although chord symbols vary considerably, a basic knowledge of the material presented here will prepare you to play the vast majority of chord symbols used today. □

Quotations and excerpts from Jazz Keyboard Harmony *by Lee Evans are used by permission.*

jazz
Improvisation
Part I —

The Classical Teacher's Guide to Easy Improvisation Techniques

BY LEE EVANS

Every pianist enjoys sitting down at a piano and being able to play without written music. Besides providing an essential motivating force for young or developing pianists, jazz improvisational techniques impart musicianship and creative skills useful to students throughout their lives as pianists.

This series of three articles looks at several techniques that a classical piano teacher, even one with little or no prior jazz experience, can use to teach students to improvise. This month focuses on melodic improvisation.

"Jazzing up" unjazzy musical material

The shift of accent from a normally strong beat to a normally weak beat — syncopation — is an extremely important characteristic of jazz. When a

Lee Evans graduated from New York's High School of Music and Art, then completed degrees at New York University and Columbia University where he received his Master of Arts and Doctor of Education. Evans, who has taught music at the junior high, high school, and college levels, plays solo piano, performs with his orchestra, and acts as pianist and musical coordinator for such performers as Tom Jones, Carol Channing, Emerson Lake and Palmer, and others.

The particular type of syncopation described above is called *accent displacement*. Some people call it accent on the offbeat, because offbeat is another way of saying weak beat.

To become more familiar with shifting the accent from stronger to weaker beats, students should practice all scales in two ways:

from The Easy-Piano Jazz Rhythm Primer *by Lee Evans. Used by permission.*

A second way to jazz up musical material is to create *anticipations of the beat*. Instead of:

Play:

A third way is to play with *detached touch* instead of legato (especially at phrase endings). Instead of:

Play:

A further way to give music a jazz feel combines all of the above suggestions. Instead of:

Play:

Instead of:

measure of music contains four beats, the first and third beats (strong beats) are usually emphasized, and the second and fourth beats (weak beats) are deemphasized. To give musical material a jazzy feel, place accents on normally weak beats or weak parts of beats, and conversely, remove accents from normally strong beats, creating the essence of syncopation.

Play the following C major scale, for example. Make those notes with an accent mark slightly louder than those notes without an accent.

A jazz pianist playing the same scale, however, would syncopate it by moving the accents to the weak beats, so that the scale would sound like this:

Play:

Students will love transforming the classical melodies of their regular piano studies into jazz expressions in the manner illustrated above. When assigning this challenge, instruct students to write as well as play their efforts. This will give them practice notating music and also enable them to experience the craft of music composition and arranging. When reviewing students' work, teachers should teach and correct such basics as stem direction, the correct shape of rests, and the notation of dynamics, accents, staccatos, and phrase marks where necessary to enhance the jazz effect.

Until students have gained confidence in their own creative abilities, it is advantageous to have them do all improvisation assignments as composition assignments. Apart from developing the useful ability to notate music, this approach avoids the problem of classically trained students who often freeze when asked to improvise in the presence of others. Once students have developed self-confidence in a compositional framework, then the improvisational, spontaneous creation of music will soon follow.

If a student is capable of improvising successfully from the outset, teachers are well advised in any event to teach compositional skills and techniques at the same time. Such an approach develops students' overall musicianship and music-writing ability and gives them such basic compositional and improvisational ideas and materials as repetition, sequence, altered forms of repetition and sequence, melodic and rhythmic augmentation and diminution, ornamentation, embellishment, and other important techniques of melodic and harmonic development.

Blue notes

Twelve-bar blues structure, demonstrated in the following improvisation example, is the most important jazz form. An integral part of all jazz improvisations, blue notes are pervasive in 12-bar blues improvisation.

Improvisational Example

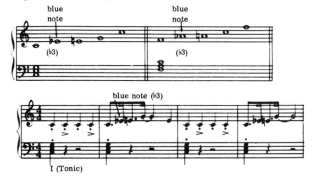

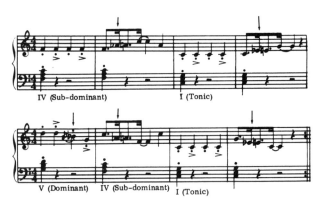

It is possible to improvise (compose) your own right hand with the given bass pattern, using chord tones, the flatted third, and any rhythm patterns of your choice:

from Beginning Jazz Improvisation by Lee Evans. Used by permission.

Once students have successfully mastered this assignment in C major, ask them to improvise (compose) other pieces in other keys, again combining one blue note (the flatted third) with chord tones, in blues structure. To accomplish this, students must first determine which are the I, IV, and V chords (12-bar blues structure chords) in the new key, and identify the flatted third for each of these chords. This offers the added educational advantage of assisting students in understanding and practicing the basic principles of transposition.

Next, have students combine two blue notes (♭3, ♭5) with chord tones, in blues structure. Again, work in several different keys.

Finally, have students combine all three blue notes (♭3, ♭5, ♭7) with chord tones, in blues structure. This, too, students should work out in several keys.

Tetrachords and the 12-bar blues structure

Lower and upper jazz tetrachords are each groupings of four tones commonly used in combination in jazz:

Jazz tetrachords in C major

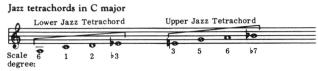

By using only these melodic tones, students can develop improvisations with a traditional jazz sound. Working first with the lower jazz tetrachords, have the student improvise (compose) a melody using only the four tones of the lower jazz tetrachord in C major (tonic), F major (sub-dominant), and G major (dominant), wherever these chords appear in blues progression in the key of C major:

Lower jazz tetrachords

C MAJOR (tonic):   F MAJOR (sub-dominant):   G MAJOR (dominant):

scale degree: 6 1 2 ♭3   6 1 2 ♭3   6 1 2 ♭3

Blues progression: I⁷ (C⁷)

IV⁷ (F⁷)

I⁷ (C⁷)   V⁷ (G⁷)

IV⁷ (F⁷)   I⁷ (C⁷)

Now improvise (compose) your own:

I⁷ (C⁷)

Next, consider the upper jazz tetrachords plus tonic. Improvise (compose) a melody using only the four tones of the upper jazz tetrachord plus the tonic tone of each chord in C major (tonic), F major (sub-dominant), and G major (dominant), wherever those chords appear in blues progression in the key of C major:

Upper jazz tetrachord (plus tonic):

C Major: F Major: G Major:

scale degree: 3 5 6 ♭7 8   3 5 6 ♭7 8   3 5 6 ♭7 8

Improvisational Example:

Blues progression: I⁷ (C⁷)

IV⁷ (F⁷)

Now improvise (compose) your own:

etc.

Last, combine lower and upper jazz tetrachords. Improvise (compose) a melody using the tones from both the lower and upper jazz tetrachords in C major (tonic), F major (sub-dominant), and G major (dominant), wherever those chords appear in blues progression in the key of C major:

Upper jazz tetrachords

C MAJOR: F MAJOR: G MAJOR:

scale degree: 3 5 6 ♭7   3 5 6 ♭7   3 5 6 ♭7

Lower jazz tetrachord

C MAJOR: F MAJOR: G MAJOR:

scale degree: 6 1 2 ♭3   6 1 2 ♭3   6 1 2 ♭3

Improvisational Example:

Blues progression: I⁷ (C⁷)

etc.

Now improvise (compose) your own:

etc.

I⁷ (C⁷)

from The Jazz Tetrachord Approach to Keyboard Jazz Improvisation *by Lee Evans. Used by permission.*

After students have completed these assignments successfully, ask them to improvise (or compose) in other keys, using tones from the lower and upper jazz tetrachords. Students must first determine which are blues progression chords in the new key, and then which tones make up their lower and upper jazz tetrachords. Also encourage your students to create new bass patterns.

There is an interesting historical sidelight to the jazz tetrachord approach to improvisation. The suggestions in this article are based upon the findings of the late Winthrop Sargeant, author of *Jazz, Hot and Hybrid* (Third edition, Da Capo Press, New York, 1975), who examined performances on the recordings of famous jazz performers (Bessie Smith, Louis Armstrong, and so on) to the mid 1930s. Sargeant's analyses revealed that these performers were all using jazz tetrachord tones in more or less the same ways. Interestingly, jazz tetrachords use the flatted third and flatted seventh degrees, but not the flatted fifth. This can be explained by the fact that prior to the 1940s — the be-bop era in jazz — the flatted fifth was not used as often as it has been since.

In the December issue Part II of Lee Evans' series will discuss jazz accompaniment styles.

Jazz Improvisation
Part II

A Classical Teacher's Guide to Jazz Accompaniment Techniques

BY LEE EVANS

Accompaniment Techniques

The pianist can achieve effective keyboard jazz accompaniment skills more readily if he is first made aware of the basic functions of accompaniments. An examination of a broad range of classical and jazz piano literature reveals four major functions of accompaniments: indicating harmonic structure; giving music rhythmic definition and impetus; filling periods of melodic inactivity; and providing contrapuntal melodic material (sounding a second melody along with the first).

Harmonic Structure

An accompaniment needs to delineate clearly the harmonic structure of a musical composition:

Lee Evans graduated from New York's High School of Music and Art, then completed degrees at New York University and Columbia University where he received his Master of Arts and Doctor of Education. Evans, who has taught music at the junior high, high school, and college levels, plays solo piano, performs with his orchestra, and acts as pianist and musical coordinator for such performers as Tom Jones, Carol Channing, Emerson, Lake and Palmer, and others.

Blues structure
chords: I
        (Tonic)

The accompaniment may also anticipate the beat:

I anticipation of 3rd beat

Or it may delay the beat:

I delay of 3rd beat

The accompaniment may be a combination of these techniques:

I (anticipation) (ant.) (pulsating on accented beats) (delay)

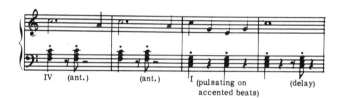

IV (ant.) (ant.) I (pulsating on accented beats) (delay)

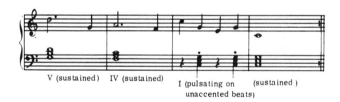

V (sustained) IV (sustained) I (pulsating on unaccented beats) (sustained)

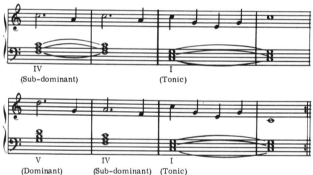

IV (Sub-dominant) I (Tonic)

V (Dominant) IV (Sub-dominant) I (Tonic)

Accompaniment Rhythms

A jazz accompaniment may be sustained, as in the previous example, or it may give rhythmic impetus, as in the examples that follow:

The accompaniment may pulsate on normally accented beats (not jazzy):

I

Or it may pulsate on normally unaccented beats (jazzier):

I

Improvise (compose) your own left hand accompaniment to the following melody in blues progression; use any combination of techniques: sustained, pulsating on accented and unaccented beats, anticipation of the beat, and delay of the beat.

I

Accompaniment Fill-Ins

Accompaniments sometimes serve to fill periods of melodic inactivity. (In such situations, the rhythmic pulse is often somewhat compromised, the pulse being implied rather than clearly indicated.) Pianists usually employ this type of accompaniment when they play with a small combo or a big band. In those settings, instruments such as trumpets and saxophones play the melody, so the pianist would not want or need to duplicate that function. In addition, instruments such as bass and drums free the pianist of having to play the bass line or of carrying the rhythmic burden. All that remains for the pianist, then, is to interject a chord here or there, in the following manner:

Create your own left-hand accompaniment that acts primarily to fill periods of melodic inactivity. Pretend that your left hand is a pianist playing with a combo (played by your right hand):

As a general rule, jazz accompaniments should be restrained (less busy) when the melody is active and more assertive (busier) when the melody is less active. It is advisable to allow melody and accompaniment to have brief simultaneous periods of inactivity, comparable to the pauses that characterize speech and conversation. Judicious use of short periods of silence or inactivity in jazz are signs of musical taste and maturity.

Include one or more examples of at least two beats of silence with the accompaniment you create to the following melody. Your accompaniment should at times employ some or all of the following techniques: indicating the pulse, sustaining the chord, or both; anticipating and delaying the beat; filling periods of melodic inactivity.

Here is my realization of the preceding exercise. (Note the use of inversions in the left hand to achieve smoother voice-leading between corresponding chords.)

Contrapuntal Melodic Material

An accompaniment may combine sustained tones and metrical ones to indicate harmonic structure and at the same time give more precise rhythmic definition and impetus to the music; it can also provide a melodic line in counterpoint:

Create your own left-hand accompaniment by combining sustained tones with metrical ones and in doing so provide a contrapuntal melodic line where you deem it appropriate:

from *Learning To Improvise Jazz Accompaniments* by Lee Evans. Used by permission.

Effective jazz performance requires mastery of both melodic and accompaniment skills. Some of the most famous and well-respected jazz pianists, such as Dave Brubeck, Bill Evans, and Count Basie, made great contributions and innovations in accompaniment techniques.

Watch for Part III of Lee Evans's jazz series in the January issue.

Jazz

Improvisation Part III —

BY LEE EVANS

The Classical Teacher's Guide to Chord Improvisation

Many people think of jazz improvisation solely as melodic variations on a theme, to borrow a phrase from the classical vernacular, but, in fact, an essential element of effective jazz improvisation is chord improvisation — the mastery and manipulation of chords. The principal elements in this fundamental pillar of jazz keyboard harmony are voice-leading and chord substitution.

Voice-Leading

The decision to play a triad or chord in root position or in any of its inversions depends upon chord spacing (voicing) and voice-leading (the movement from one tone to another in each of various voice parts). General principles of voice-leading, drawn from both classical music and, to a degree, jazz, are stepwise motion in preference to wide leaps and stationary or contrary motion in at least one voice in relation to the others. Though pre-20th-century classical music voice-leading rules often prohibit parallel fifths and parallel octaves, these parallel intervals are completely acceptable in jazz. Generally speaking, voice-leading is smoothest when the inner voices are less active than outer voices.

Compare the following:

Lee Evans graduated from New York's High School of Music and Art, then completed degrees at New York University and Columbia University where he received his Master of Arts and Doctor of Education. Evans, who has taught music at the junior high, high school, and college levels, plays solo piano, performs with his orchestra, and acts as pianist and musical coordinator for such performers as Tom Jones, Carol Channing, Emerson, Lake, and Palmer, and others.

Correct but awkward voice-leading:

(wide leaps)
root position triads

Better voice-leading:

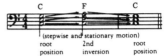

(stepwise and stationary motion)
root   2nd   root
position   inversion   position

Playing the F major chord in an inversion rather than in root position improves the voice-leading.

In the following example, the left hand maintains root position while the right hand inverts the F major triad.

Correct but awkward voice-leading:

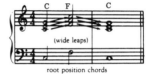

(wide leaps)

root position chords

Better voice-leading:

(stepwise and stationary motion)

root position chords

Closely tied to voice-leading are two other aspects of keyboard jazz: motion and a sense of continuity created by avoiding or delaying a feeling of finality. This may be accomplished in several different ways — rhythmically, melodically, texturally, and dynamically — but one of the basic ways is harmonically.

Music of the 17th, 18th, and 19th centuries used as its harmonic basis chord progressions with clearly understood functions that gave the music direction; for example, the function of dominant resolving to tonic imparts a sense of motion. A great deal of 20th-century music, including jazz, also uses this phenomenon of chordal progressions to develop musical motion. Though sometimes chords are simply enjoyable as sound-entities unto themselves and do not involve any sense of function or direction, harmonic chordal improvisation depends on the creation of a sense of inevitable movement, flow, and continuity, and with the way the keyboard jazz artist creates smooth, directed musical flow.

Certain tones in diatonic music contain properties of rest and others of motion. Rest tones, those with a sense of finality, sound as though they need not progress to other tones, although they may comfortably move to other rest tones. Generally, the first, third, fifth, and eighth degrees of the major or minor scale (the notes of the fundamental triad) are considered rest tones. Motion tones sound as though they must progress to the nearest rest tones, generally the second degree of the scale, which moves to the first or third degree; the fourth degree of the scale, which moves to the third; the

sixth scale degree, which moves to the fifth; and the seventh degree, which moves to the eighth.

C Major (numbers represent scale degrees)

motion rest   motion rest   motion rest   motion rest
tone   tones   tone   tone   tone   tone   tone   tone

Play the following G♭$^9_7$ chord on the piano and pause:

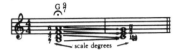

Your ear should tell you that the G$^9_7$ chord, composed entirely of motion tones, demands resolution to the C triad, composed entirely of rest tones. This example shows that one of the most effective ways to achieve a sense of continuity and flow in music is by using motion tones. Conversely, to achieve a sense of finality, rest tones should be used.

Two all-too-frequent performing errors relate to this motion tone/rest tone issue. The first is overusing root position chords, which results in poor voice-leading and the feeling that the music lacks a sense of direction. Root position chords have a final sound; for example, the following root position chord does not sound as though it must progress to another chord:

On the other hand, an inversion sounds as though it must progress to other chords en route to root position:

The second performance flaw involves using too many rest tones and too few motion tones. The basic triad is composed of rest tones that do not offer the sense that they must resolve to other tones. Other tones in this scale, however, do create the sense that they must resolve, or move, to another tone:

The following example, the Rodgers and Hart song "Manhattan," demonstrates the inadequacy of using too many root position and too few motion tones.

from Jazz Keyboard Harmony by Lee Evans. Used by permission.

A more satisfying harmonization of the same song illustrates more frequent use of inversions and of added-tone chords (chords that contain motion tones); the result is a greater sense of flow and continuity than in the root-position version. This harmonization creates the feeling that at every step of the way another chord must follow; thus, the arrangement avoids a sense of finality and creates a forward thrust. (In this example notice the avoidance of root position.)

Teachers should use the following procedure when showing students how to create smoother voice-leading by inverting chords.

Have students play all the chords of a given chord progression in root position with the left hand alone.

Using the same chord symbols, have the student play left-hand chords, incorporating a mixture of root positions and inversions to achieve smoother voice-leading.

Again, with the same chord symbols and with the bass line given, add right-hand chords in a jazz rhythm using the principles of desirable voice-leading.

Here is one possible realization of the chord symbols given above:

Chord Substitution

Experienced jazz pianists use various chord substitution techniques to create more idiomatic sounds and to generate greater harmonic interest than those chords found in traditional sheet music or in lead sheets (single melody lines with chord symbols — lead sheets appear in fake books, so called because "fake" is synonymous with "improvise" in jazz terminology). Most experienced jazz pianists use substitute chords by instinct rather than by conscious choice; interestingly, as good as the best jazz pianists' instincts are, if these musicians are asked to explain the techniques they use, they probably cannot offer either an explanation or insight into the subject. These techniques can be formally taught and learned, however, as shown in the following example, which explains the most frequently used substitution technique — circle-of-fifths substitution.

In the circle of fifths, the keys of the major scales are arranged clockwise in ascending fifths, with the number of sharps in each succeeding scale increasing by one. Examine the circle counterclockwise and the arrangement of the major scale keys is by descending fifths, with the number of flats in each succeeding scale increasing by one.

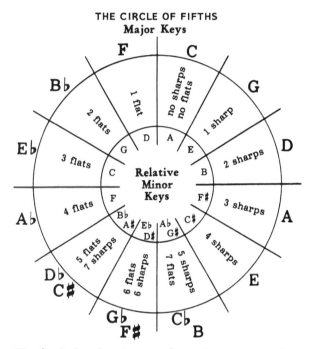

THE CIRCLE OF FIFTHS
Major Keys

To find the dominant of any key, proceed one step clockwise through the circle. To find the secondary dominant (the dominant of the dominant), proceed an additional clockwise step.

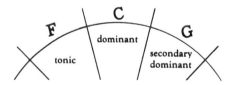

To apply circle-of-fifths substitution techniques to the following progression:

| C / / / | F / / / |

First identify the dull section or the passage with the chords you wish to change. For example, a more interesting progression would replace the C chord in the first measure; in this case the very next chord is the destination chord.

| C / / / | F / / / |
change   destination chord

Work backwards from the destination chord (F in this example), going clockwise through the circle of fifths to find the dominant seventh (C7).

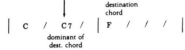

Work further backwards from the destination chord, going clockwise through the circle of fifths to locate the secondary dominant of the destination chord.

```
                          destination
                          chord
| G₇  /  C⁷ /  | F  /  /  /  |
secondary
dominant
of dest. chord
```

Change the secondary dominant to minor seventh (G7 becomes Gm7), because jazz pianists almost invariably and instinctively try to create ii7-V7-I progressions.

```
substitute chords ┌──── destination
                       chord
| Gm7  /  C7  /  | F  /  /  /  |
  ii7        V7      I
```

This ii7-V7-I progression occurs so frequently in jazz that it is perhaps the most important of all jazz chord progressions; practicing it in descending and ascending half-step and whole-step patterns, as in the following exercises, will prove extremely useful.

To practice ascending half-step patterns, read the previous exercises backwards, as follows:

To work on descending and ascending whole-step patterns, read every other bar of the previous exercises:

ascending (both hands)

etc.

I Can't Get Started (original:)   Ira Gershwin/Vernon Duke

from Jazz Keyboard Harmony by Lee Evans/E.B. Marks-Belwin Mills.

Consider another example of circle-of-fifths substitution in the following progression, which, coincidentally, happens to be the same chord progression as measures 1-5 of the song "Tea for Two."

| B♭m7 / E♭7 / | B♭m7 / E♭7 / | A♭M7 / A♭6 / |
| A♭M7 / A♭6 / | B♭m7

As before, identify the dull harmonic progression you want to change and refer to the very next chord as the destination chord.

| B♭m7 / E♭7 / | B♭m7 / E♭7 /

           change   destination chord
| A♭M7 / A♭6 / | A♭M7 / A♭6 / | B♭m7

Work backwards from the destination chord, going clockwise through the circle of fifths to find its dominant seventh.

| B♭m7 / E♭7 / | B♭m7 / E♭7 / | A♭M7 / A♭6 / |

                    destination chord
| A♭M7 / F7 / | B♭m7
           V7   i

Work backwards from the destination chord, going further clockwise through the circle of fifths to find the secondary dominant.

| B♭m7 / E♭7 / | B♭m7 / E♭7 / | A♭M7 / A♭6 / |

                 destination chord
| C7 / F7 / | B♭m7
  II7   V7   i

Change the secondary dominant to minor seventh (C7 becomes Cm7).

| B♭m7 / E♭7 / | B♭m7 / E♭7 / | A♭M7 / A♭6 / |

substitute chords   destination chord
| Cm7 / F7 / | B♭m7
  ii7   V7   i

Now play measures 1-5 of "Tea for Two," first with the original chord progression and then with the substitute chords in measure 4. You will readily hear that the substitute chords add considerable harmonic interest. Of course, in the case of "Tea for Two," the melody tones of the song do not clash with the substitute chords. When a skillful jazz pianist anticipates such a clash, he might change the melody note to match the chord tones and thus avoid unwanted dissonance.

In case you are wondering why it is necessary to work through all the intermediary steps to achieve circle-of-fifths substitution when you can simply think of ii7-V7-I, consider the following example. If you were to keep going further backwards from the destination chord, you would wind up "out of key:"

Identify the progression to change and refer to the very next chord as the destination chord:

           change   destination chord
| C / Am / | Dm7 / G7 / |

As before, substitute by referring to the circle of fifths:

              destination chord
| C / Em7 A7 | Dm7 / G7 / |
        ii7   V7   i

Repeat the substitution process, with Em7 as the new destination chord:

          new destination chord   original destination chord
| F♯m7 B7   Em7 A7 | Dm7 / G7 / |
  ii7   V7   i
         ii7   V7   i
substitute chords —— 3 ——

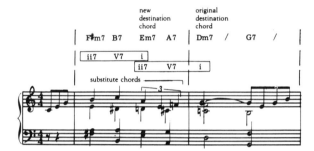

By going further backwards in the circle of fifths from the destination chord, we wound up being "out of key," in the sense that the F♯m-B7 progression does not suggest the tonality of the piece, C major. Compare the above substitute chords version of "I Can't Get Started" with the original. Here again, you will readily hear the rich harmony that circle-of-fifths chord substitution creates.

To take circle-of-fifths substitution a step further, consider the situation of an isolated dominant seventh chord: | F7 / / / |
      V7

Here the music can be enriched harmonically as before by working backwards from an imaginary destination chord (the tonic of F7, or B♭), going clockwise through the circle of fifths to identify the secondary dominant of B♭ (C7), which changes to minor seventh (Cm7) to create a ii7-V7 progression:

          change   imaginary destination chord
| F7 / / / | B♭ to | C7 / F7 / | B♭ to | Cm7 / F7 / | B♭
  V7   I   II7   V7   I   ii7   V7   I

In other words, any dominant seventh can be preceded by the secondary dominant made minor to create a ii7-V7 progression.

Chord manipulation is a significant area of study for the aspiring jazz pianist. These tools and techniques of chord substitution and harmonic improvisation are completely compatible with classical teaching methods. All classical piano teachers, even those with limited or no prior jazz experience, can use them to motivate their students.

Jazzing It Up in Style (Guidelines for Keyboard Jazz Performance)

by Lee Evans

At jazz master classes I ask pianists to play any two popular songs and then to improvise, using each song as a framework for the improvisation. My critiques are based on certain generally accepted criteria of jazz performance. Using the guidelines given below, teachers can heighten aspiring jazz pianists' awareness of the elements of keyboard jazz performance and provide them with a basis for future self-evaluation and improvement.

Stylistic originality, while difficult to achieve, is a certain road to recognition and success in the jazz field. Many pianists emulate the famous jazz piano styles of performers such as Erroll Garner, George Shearing, and Art Tatum.

Unfortunately, these players often fail to develop a musical signature of their own, or to modify and refine famous styles into individual stylistic statements. Although stylistic consistency can sometimes bore the listener because of its inherent lack of variety, stylistic eclecticism often reflects indecisiveness and lack of originality.

One element of style a few great jazz pianists have mastered is *harmonic originality.* For example, the impact of chord enrichment is especially powerful in the playing of the late Bill Evans.

Locked-hands style of George Shearing:

Famous Jazz Piano Styles by Lee Evans

Harmonic style of Bill Evans:

Chord progressions should be logical and satisfying, employing substitutions when appropriate. Rather than rigidly playing root-position chords, pianists should choose chord inversions that will produce smoother, more acceptable voice-leading. Motion tones (those tones contained in altered chords and other added-tone chords) may be inserted to supplement rest tones (those tones contained in the basic triad). Current harmonic language — extended harmony, quartal harmony, polytonality — can prevent pianists from getting stuck in the rut of the older, more traditional harmonic vocabulary.

Melodic improvisation should be characterized by purposeful use of scale tones and chord tones. Tones that stray from the underlying chords should be used mindfully; used incorrectly, they sound like mistakes. Purposely and skillfully playing outside the chord produces desirable dissonances characteristic of contemporary jazz performance.

Wrong note (clashes with underlying chord)

Correct note (matches underlying chord)

Purposeful use of wrong note (made correct through its use as an embellishing tone)

Much of today's melodic improvisation features chaconne improvisation — continuous melodic variation over a harmonic pattern that has no recurring or recognizable melody. Many jazz performers avoid the more challenging passacaglia improvisation — continuous variation based on a recognizable, recurring theme — an approach that requires greater improvisational skill. To develop a theme melodically, performers need to master such compositional techniques as *repetition and sequence, rhythmic and melodic diminution and augmentation,* and *ornamentation and embellishment.* The following melodic reference uses ornamentation and embellishment. Notice that each note of the given motive is present in the embellished version.

Given

Embellished

Many jazz players learn to improvise by deliberately memorizing standard jazz phrase patterns. When they employ these patterns in improvisation they usually mix a portion of one phrase with a portion of another:

On the surface the most impressive jazz improvisers are those who have built the largest vocabulary of such established jazz phrases in all keys and who have a keen feeling for when to employ and how to manipulate this vocabulary. These jazz practitioners often overlook an important area of improvisation, however, the manipulation of the melodic line accomplished through motivic development:

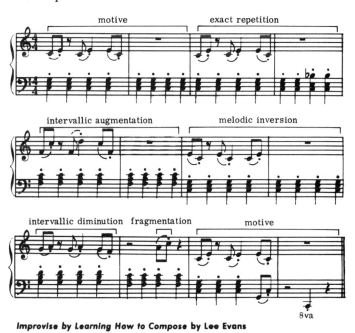

An outstanding sense of *rhythm* is the *sine qua non* of respected jazz pianism. The pianist needs to maintain a constant, unwavering tempo, especially in unaccompanied solo-playing where there is no bassist or drummer to keep the beat. Eighth and sixteenth notes should not be rushed, and rests should receive full value. At the same time, performers should also strive for rhythmic variety; the best jazz improvisations are marked by wide rhythmic scope.

Phrase structure contributes significantly to effective jazz performance. For example, Oscar Peterson's distinctive jazz style owes much to the extended phrase; at just the moment that the listener would expect one of Peterson's phrases to end — to take a breath, so to speak — he extends the phrase to breathless lengths. His improvisations are characterized by lucid organization and separation of musical phrases. Virtually any recording by Peterson will illustrate this point.

In addition to style, harmony, melody, rhythm, and phrase structure, several other aspects of jazz performance deserve attention:

Articulation — accuracy in execution and appropriate use of *legato, portato,* and *staccato;* full use of dynamic range

Keyboard range — use of all 88 keys

Pedaling and touch — intelligent use of the sostenuto pedal; using appropriate keyboard touch

Right-hand and left-hand functions — use of each hand for melodic improvisation as well as for chordal accompaniment. The right hand should at times be used for chording and the left for melodic purposes — a reversal of traditional hand roles — or, both hands may employ mixed roles:

Usual hand roles; melody in R.H. chords in L.H.

Reversal of roles; chords in R.H. melody in L.H.

Mixed hand roles melody and chord tones in each hand

Hopefully, this analysis of keyboard jazz performance will offer pianists fundamental criteria for setting self-improvement standards and provide piano teachers with jazz-listening guidelines.

All examples are published by Edward B. Marks Music Corp./Hal Leonard Publishing Corporation. Used by permission.

Lee Evans received his bachelor's degree from New York University and his M.A. and Ph.D. in Music Education from Columbia University. He has taught at the junior high, high school, and college levels. Currently Lee Evans writes teaching books on jazz for the Hal Leonard Company and serves as musical coordinator for Tom Jones.

Popular Music in Music Education

Lee Evans

Lee Evans has written an extremely comprehensive series of books about popular music.

The materials and performance techniques of popular music are not traditionally utilized or taught in piano pedagogy. Popular music, by definition, has wide appeal and for this reason among others, must be considered a valuable tool for music educators.

The term "popular music," usually taken to include virtually all kinds of music other than classical music, is an unfortunate and too comprehensive term, as many categories of music to which the term ordinarily applies and which should be considered individually are grouped together—jazz, rock, country, gospel, folk, pop, etc. Moreover, the word 'popular' is often used in a pejorative sense by the classical cognoscente to describe musical styles that, partly because of their lack of complexity, have had immediate comprehensibility and mass appeal at their time throughout the ages. Furthermore, popular music, ever-changing and redefined by each succeeding generation, is thought of as having a limited life span whereas classical music has had a more enduring quality. (Why musical expressions which have had immediacy of appeal to the masses have not demonstrated survivability as important works of art, has, to the knowledge of this writer, never been satisfactorily explained.)

Although it is difficult to define, popular music clearly has many technical and aesthetic elements in common with classical music. Both share a common written language containing such features as melody, harmony and rhythm. In other respects, however, distinct differences exist and may be easily identified.

An important aspect of popular music is melody without further thematic development, generally resulting in works of modest length. Successful development requires a high degree of compositional craftsmanship, the ability to manipulate and shape small amounts of musical clay into a musical sculpture larger and more significant than the sum of its parts. But the composing of popular music also requires great skill, particularly melodic and rhythmic skill.

Another basic distinction between popular music and classical music is the fact that popular materials are not inviolable as are classical materials in today's musical climate. In other words, it is acceptable for a pop singer to change notes in performing a Cole Porter composition, but it is not acceptable for a lieder singer to alter Schubert. (This has not always been the case; prior to the early 1900s renowned pianists would not have hesitated to change the score for dramatic effect in performing a classical work.) Popular materials have always served as the framework within which the interpreter is expected to take unrestricted liberties. The interpretation, therefore, is of the essence in popular music whereas the composition is in classical music. It is even possible to argue that it matters little in classical music if a performer deviates from the "correct" interpretation, for the composition always remains in its purity to be interpreted as the composer intended. In popular music, however, *every* interpretation is definitive, a new product for better or worse.

In fact, it is this very newness and freshness that characterizes jazz, one genre of popular music. In jazz improvisation, repeating oneself constitutes a violation of the spirit and purpose of the idiom, a violation that quickly results in the consignment of such a musician to musical purgatory. This purgatory consists of disrespect by peers and audiences and a subsequent inability to secure employment in the field.

Improvisation is not a new technique nor is it exclusively indigenous to jazz or other popular forms; the Baroque era with its figured bass was a precursor. (In a period even earlier than that, improvisation was instrumental in the emergence of a more melismatic Gregorian chant.) What is new is the realization that jazz improvisation and other techniques of jazz performance can be taught. What is also new is that materials which teach jazz are being produced at a phenomenal rate. Finally, what is new is that classical teachers are discovering that they can teach jazz and other forms of popular music without having to become accomplished performers in these idioms. This writer takes issue with the widely held view that possession of a knack for jazz performance is dependent upon a divine gift. It has been demonstrated that jazz can be broken down into identifiable components and successfully taught in a methodical manner with the authenticity, skill and discipline ordinarily associated with the teaching of classical music.

What is the main objective of music instruction? As most students will not make music a career, one of the principal goals must be to impart basic musical tools which students may employ for enrichment and pleasure. Two such important tools are improvisation and sightreading. Proficiency in these areas will enable students to enjoy music with greater success as an avocation. We have all met people who express regret at having abandoned lessons too early, thus precluding any possibility that they might pursue music as a hobby. Ideally, teachers have the obligation to provide materials and to teach students techniques that will motivate them to continue their keyboard training.

Jazz and other popular music expressions have tremendous relevance to students. All music educators, therefore, should consider including popular materials as part of an overall music curriculum. Such materials are valuable in imparting a feeling for these idioms as well as aiding the student in the development of technical keyboard skills and the learning of sophisticated musicological concepts. Furthermore, these materials offer motivational value to stem the tide of dropouts in keyboard education.

In a November 1969 article in Music Educators Journal ("Youth Music In Education"), an authority offered the following insight:

> [To study only] ... the masters is as absurd as permitting only Euripides, Shakespeare and Moliere to be performed in the theater. Music education must encompass all music. If student musical attitudes are to be affected by music education, the music teacher's openness to new music serves as a necessary model.

Commissioned by Clavier

BY LYNN FREEMAN OLSON

It takes only a few moments of hearing "Skateboard's" ensemble sound to realize that the talented hand of a real pro has been at work here. In the field of easy jazz piano pedagogy material, many practitioners have proved themselves experts at explaining jazz, composing clever numbers, and knowing how to write for different levels; they have given us a variety of publications to satisfy many tastes. When you see names such as Tony Caramia, Jerry Coker, Ann Collins, Lee Evans, or Alan Swain (list necessarily abbreviated due to space) on the covers of musical publications, you can assure yourself that inside you are going to encounter some good jazz sounds suitable for basic piano instruction. In my opinion Lee Evans heads the list of these educational jazz composers.

Jazz composers writing for young people are in essence "fighting a snake." Jazz is improvisational by nature, and a lot of its feel is not always natural to today's children, who hear vastly different styles in their popular music. (Remember not to judge — listen and learn!) Keyboard jazz's historical significance, however, ensures that its traditions continue as part of today's tapestry of sounds.

We beg to have jazz notated for us and the pupils we teach, but therein lies some problem, because to teach jazz is to teach improvisation — at least, that should be the case — based on knowledge of harmony and a collection of conventional musical fragments, phrases, and progressions that should be fairly automatic at the keyboard. In fact, many traditional keyboard styles comprise the complete jazz picture. I always suggest teachers study jazz playing if they want to include it at all in the studio experience.

Having listed all of my precautions, I will now say, "Relax." Many fine books full of jazz flavor and simple techniques are available for us to use. "Skateboard" is from Evans's collection *Jazzmatazz*. Each piece in it has a teacher accompaniment, but it includes no methodology; Evans has published numerous other books for that purpose. *Jazzmatazz* offers just winsome and ear-tickling pieces.

In "Skateboard" you can observe representative elements of the book. Foremost is the use of the eighth notes played long-short as jazz triplets. Note that a typical jazz player would automatically swing the eighths in this manner, whether or not the direction to do so appeared on the piece. This jazz feel is fairly easy to convey — just demonstrate it. Once the swinging sound gets in the ear and hand, even your young rockers reared on a straight, evenly accented four or eight to the segment will catch the natural, relaxed appeal.

One challenging aspect of "Skateboard" is the way the student has to begin it with just the half-note beat while the teacher plays off-beats and a syncopated dominant. Be sure you establish a secure pulse between you. The pupil needs to observe the staccato indications carefully because these releases are typical in jazz. Also, you can properly refer to the flatted fifth in both student and teacher parts as a blue note. The piece also demonstrates what is known as a walking bass, which imitates a bass fiddle part. This ostinato effect is a real aid to the jazz beginner when he is first establishing the necessary hand independence.

Enjoy the sounds of "Skateboard" and of the entire *Jazzmatazz* collection. In other words, relax, follow Evans, and swing along.

Lee Evans might never have entered the field of piano education as fully as he has. His activities as a jazz-pop recording artist, show musical director and contractor, touring jazz performer playing the best clubs, and a pianist featured on television might have been enough for any other person. Yet on the inside Evans is a teacher; he possesses the basic need and ability to instruct and help make the paths of jazz and pop music easier for students and their teachers to traverse. A solid citizen of Music Mecca (New York City), Evans has been at the very heart of commercial music, creating and producing it for many years. He is among those who underpins his talents with a solid educational base, having earned a masters and a doctorate from Columbia University, and he has put this to work in the classroom, both in public schools and colleges, as well as on stages, in recording studios, and in front of cameras. His work is a happy and successful blend of the reality of commercial music and the comprehensive theoretical knowledge so necessary to any complete musician, whether serious or pop.

Skateboard

LEE EVANS

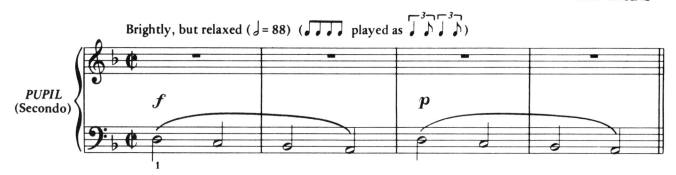

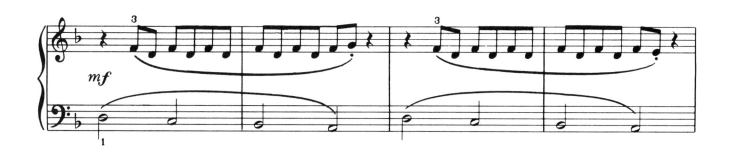

"Skateboard" is reprinted from the collection JAZZMATAZZ by Lee Evans, available from Hal Leonard Publishing Corporation, 8112 W. Bluemound Road, P.O. Box 13819, Milwaukee, Wisconsin for $3.95.

Piano Compositions by students

May-June 1987

Based on the

Learn To
COMPOSE and NOTATE SERIES
(Hal Leonard Publishing Corp.)
by
LEE EVANS and MARTHA BAKER

A Night Song Mystery

Andy Stage
May 26, 1987
age 9 3/4

Using: Motive, Repetition, Retrograde and Sequence

Cats Cruising

composed By
Ernest Cor
age 10 Date 5-

Using Motive, repetition and, sequ
and retrograde

CANDY CANE BLUES

Composed by
Alison Rice
5-12-87
Age 13

Using basic 12-bar blues chord progression, sequence, and syncopation

Bumblebee Bop-Hop

Elizabeth Mui
May 6 1987
age: 15

Dedicated to:
Neysa Sterner

using 12 bar blues chord progression, seque
and sincopation

REVIEWS REVIEWS REVIEWS REVIEWS REVIEWS REVIEWS

By Julia Amada-Adams

LEARN TO COMPOSE AND NOTATE MUSIC AT THE KEYBOARD and **LEARN TO HARMONIZE AND TRANSPOSE AT THE KEYBOARD, Lee Evans/Martha Baker.** Lee Evans and Martha Baker have written two books which will soon become an important part of the teaching studio. *Learn To Compose And Notate Music* and *Learn To Harmonize And Transpose* provide the teacher with a systematic presentation of elementary skills needed in learning how to compose, notate, harmonize, and transpose. By using a creative approach, elementary students are immediately involved in composing. The beginning level of *Learning To Compose And Notate* introduces the student to repetition, sequence, retrograde, and inversion, but leaves teaching the "writing" aspects of notation to the teacher (direction of stems, shape of rests, dynamics, etc.). For each of the four forms introduced, a simple motive is provided which is then changed to demonstrate the form (sequence, etc.). Following each example, the student is then asked to write original endings to the melodies, using the form described or a combination of forms. The motives presented for study are very short (one to four bars) and technically very easy so the student can devote full attention to understanding the form presented. By the end of the book, students are writing entire pieces using all of the forms discussed. An appendix is provided to describe "altered" forms of repetition and sequence. The description of rhythmic diminution and augmentation, interval diminution and augmentation, melodic alteration, rhythmic shift, and octave displacement are simply and clearly explained with musical examples of each.

Learn To Harmonize And Transpose offers eleven organized "theory" lessons which can be incorporated into private lessons. Each lesson discusses both harmonization and transposition and provides exercises which will develop skill in these areas. The format of the book includes simply presented definitions of musical terms, as well as examples as to how each is applied to harmonization and transposition. The students are taken slowly through I,i; I V7 and i V7; I IV I V7 I and i iv i V7 i. Students are asked to apply the designated chords to the melodies provided, to alter the type of harmonic patterns (variances of "on-beat" as well as "off-beat" harmonizations are offered), and to transpose each to various keys. By the time a student has completed all lessons, he/she will have attained a sound fundamental understanding of basic harmonization as well as a proficiency in applying the harmonization concepts to melodies. At $3.95 each, these books are an invaluable tool for the beginning student. (Hal Leonard Pub. Corp., Piano Plus, Inc., $3.95 each)

PIANO GUILD NOTES

✔ **(S2-4) MARTHA BAKER, Take Ten for Jazz** (teacher's manual). This manual will help you take the plunge and introduce jazz into your students' curriculum. Included are 33 ten-minute plans telling the teacher exactly what material to cover at the lesson (and how) as well as what the student's jazz assignment should be, drawing from Lee Evans's excellent publications *The Easy-Piano Jazz Rhythm Primer* and *Beginning Jazz Improvisation*, followed by *The Elements of Jazz* and *Learning to Improvise Jazz Accompaniments*. The author has based all instruction on the concept of "hear, do, and then see" in what appears to be a method that works. She also does a good job of keeping the jazz commitment limited to a brief part of traditional lesson time. Try this jazz curriculum in the middle of the year to perk up your teaching. (Hal Leonard, $5.95) J.M.

Piano Teachers:

To acquire LEE EVANS
for an all-morning workshop
for your piano teaching group,
call or write to:

Hal Leonard Corporation
7777 West Bluemound Road
Milwaukee, WI 53213
(414)774-3630

Workshop Title:
Jazz for the Classical Piano Teacher
New Concepts and Materials